TEEN STRONG

Behind the Scenes WITH

Marsai Martin

by Kristy Stark

FAST READS

full tilt PRESS

Marsai Martin
TEEN STRONG

Full Tilt Press
42964 Osgood Road
Fremont, CA 94539
readfulltilt.com

Full Tilt Press publications may be purchased for educational, business, or sales promotional use.

Editorial Credits
Design and layout by Sara Radka
Edited by Renae Gilles
Copyedited by Nikki Ramsay

Image Credits
Getty Images: Beautycon/John Sciulli, 20, Entertainment Weekly/Andrew Toth, 16, Entertainment Weekly/Neilson Barnard, 27 (bottom), EyeEm/Fabio Pagani, cover (accent), EyeEm/Wathanyu Kanthawong, 29 (bottom), iStock/choness, 17 (money), iStock/Sasha_Ka, 29 (top), iStock/the8monkey, background, Mattel UCLA Children's Hospital/Mike Windle, 8, Rodin Eckenroth, 23, Sarah Morris, 25, Secret Deodorant/Kristy Sparow, 15, TBS/Paul Zimmerman, 27 (top); Newscom: AdMedia/Birdie Thompson, 22, Everett Collection/Kristin Callahan, 3, iPhotoLive/DVSIL, 26 (bottom), MEGA/AFF-USA.com/Janet Gough, 6, MEGA/CD, 14, MEGA/Image Press Agency/Xavier Collin, 7, Polaris/PIP, 4, Sipa USA/John Salangsang, 26 (top), Splash News/PG, 10, SplashNews/imageSPACE/CraSH, 19, SplashNews/Johns PKI, 9, TNS/Atlanta Journal-Constitution/Alyssa Pointer, 11, UPI/Jim Ruymen, 12, 24, WENN.com/Nicky Nelson, 18; Shutterstock: ADragan, 17 (jar), aniok, background, Christian Delbert, 17 (typewriter), DFree, cover (main), 1, kontur-vid, 17 (chair), Ovchinnkov Vladimir, 17 (projector), VGstockstudio, 21

ISBN: 978-1-62920-843-5 (library binding)
ISBN: 978-1-62920-855-8 (ePub)

CONTENTS

Introduction 4

Getting Started 6

Becoming Teen Strong..........10

Building an Empire.................14

Work in Progress....................18

A Bright Future 22

Timeline...................................26

Quiz..28

Activity 29

Glossary...................................30

Read More 31

Internet Sites 31

Index...32

Introduction

Issa Rae and Regina Hall were Marsai's costars in *Little*.

On April 12, 2019, the movie *Little* was released in theaters. At age 14, Marsai Martin starred in the film. The teen had an added role too. She was an **executive producer** for the film. At the time it came out, she was the youngest producer to make a big-budget movie in the United States.

Marsai also came up with the idea for *Little*. She was just 10 years old at the time. She felt there weren't enough movies that told the stories of young black people.

In the film, Marsai's character deals with bullies at school. The teen used her personal life to help her play the role. Kids used to tease her. They thought she was weird. They did not understand why she often mimicked movies.

It was important for Marsai to make a movie that other people could relate to. It was also important to increase diversity in the media. Marsai is working hard to increase **representation** for people of color.

executive producer: one of the highest positions in media production; may be involved in the production process, or simply oversee it more generally

representation: the process of giving people a voice through better coverage and exposure

Getting Started

Marsai's family supports her at home, work, and during special events, including the Los Angeles premiere of *Little* in 2019.

Caila Marsai Martin was born on August 14, 2004, in Plano, Texas. Marsai uses her middle name for her acting career. But her family calls her Caila.

Marsai's parents are Joshua and Carol Martin. Before his daughter's fame, Joshua worked in auto **finance**. Now he helps run her **production company**. At first, the teen's mom was her manager. Now she helps with social media. Marsai also has a younger sister. Her name is Cydni. Marsai loves spending time with her sister. She often posts images of them together on Instagram.

At age five, Marsai started acting in TV commercials. Her first job was in ads for the Choice Hotel chain. That was just the beginning. By 2020, she had been in 14 different TV shows, shorts, and movies.

Marsai's favorite singer is Beyoncé. She met her hero at the White House in 2016.

In 2020, Marsai was added to *Forbes'* 30 Under 30, a list "spotlighting the next generation of talent."

finance: issues having to do with money and how it is spent or saved

production company: a company that is responsible for developing and filming a specific production, such as a movie or TV show

In 2015, Marsai attended the Mattel Party on the Pier in Santa Monica, California. The event raised money for the UCLA Mattel Children's Hospital.

Marsai's Beginning

Marsai's parents did not set out for her to be on TV. When Marsai was a kid, she was at a mall with her parents. They decided to do glamour shots. The photographer saw that Marsai followed directions well. He urged her parents to show the photos to **talent agencies**. The photographer promised a discount on the photos if they took his advice. Before long, Marsai had her first contract.

Later, Marsai was a student at a film school in Texas. Hollywood agent Melissa Berger saw her there. She hired Marsai to work with her talent agency.

Marsai needed to be closer to her agent. So her family moved from Texas to Southern California in 2013. In the next few months, Marsai was hired for many TV commercials.

The young actress also got a role in the *Black-ish* **pilot** for ABC. The show's creator, Kenya Barris, saw her potential. He said that she was "this pint-sized little ball of talent with these amazing glasses." Marsai was only 10 years old when they started to film.

TALENTED CO-STARS

Marsai is not the only talented teen on *Black-ish*. Miles Brown plays her twin brother. Miles is an actor, dancer, and rapper. He also goes by the name Baby Boogaloo. The teen started hip-hop dancing at age three. Later, he joined the cast of *Yo Gabba Gabba*, where he was able to show the world his acting and dancing skills.

talent agency: a company that helps find jobs for actors and other professionals in the entertainment industry

pilot: one episode of a TV show made as a trial run

Becoming Teen Strong

When Marsai first read her lines with Miles Brown, Kenya Barris thought the two "immediately . . . felt like brother and sister."

On *Black-ish*, Marsai works with an all-star cast. There are many talented teens and veteran actors. Most cast members are people of color. This team of comedians has made the show a hit. They have also built a supportive community around Marsai.

From this place of **empowerment**, Marsai and her dad **pitched** the idea for *Little* to Barris. The film was based on a 1988 movie called *Big*. The film starred Tom Hanks. In *Big*, a teenage boy wishes to be a grown-up. The next morning, he wakes up in the body of a grown man. Marsai's idea for *Little* was to have a grown woman wake up as a teenager. Barris was immediately on board with the idea for the film.

In addition to serving in politics, Stacey Abrams is an author and business leader.

In 2018, Marsai campaigned for Stacey Abrams. Abrams hoped to be the first African American governor of Georgia. At the time, Marsai was not even old enough to vote.

---

empowerment: the process of becoming more confident and taking action for oneself

pitch: to present an idea for a TV show or movie to people who could help pay for it

Kenya Barris helped Marsai and the cast of *Black-ish* accept the award for Outstanding Comedy Series at the 2015 NAACP Image Awards.

Big Ideas

Marsai's agents did not agree with Barris about *Little*. They thought that Marsai would be too busy. They said she should "just chill" during breaks from filming *Black-ish*. Also, the agents did not think there were any good movie roles for Marsai. But Marsai did not agree with their reasoning. She thought that she should create those roles instead of waiting for them to come to her. So Marsai fired her agents. She did what she knew was the right choice for her.

Marsai noticed that there were not many movies or shows that featured young people of color. She decided to do something about it. Now Marsai is changing Hollywood from the inside out. She is adding "more diversity, more inclusivity, more YA-type films that people my age can relate to," she said in 2019.

Marsai is also urging other young people to get involved in show business. "This is the next generation," Marsai said. "It's about getting Hollywood to understand us, listen to us, and follow in our footsteps."

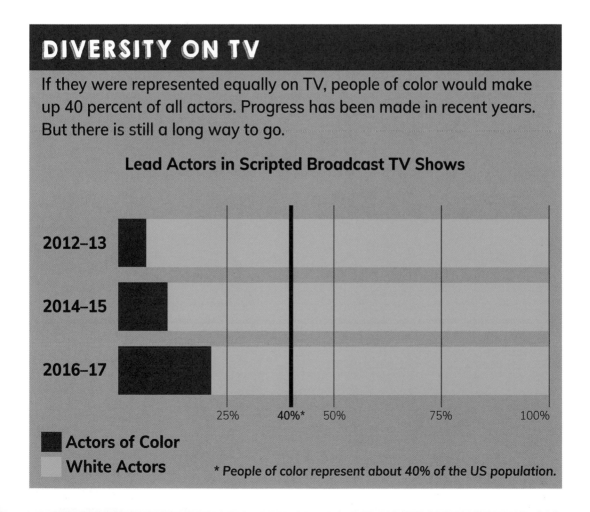

DIVERSITY ON TV

If they were represented equally on TV, people of color would make up 40 percent of all actors. Progress has been made in recent years. But there is still a long way to go.

Lead Actors in Scripted Broadcast TV Shows

2012–13

2014–15

2016–17

25%   40%*   50%   75%   100%

■ Actors of Color
□ White Actors

People of color represent about 40% of the US population.

Building an Empire

On *Black-ish*, Marsai is part of an ensemble cast. This means many actors are featured equally. Marsai shares screen time with Laurence Fishburne, Marcus Scribner, Anthony Anderson, and Tracee Ellis Ross, among others.

While most teens her age are busy with homework and hobbies, Marsai is busy building an **empire**. Her work is expanding into music, business, beauty, and fashion.

Marsai is multitalented. Most people know her for her acting roles. But the teen is also a singer. In 2016, she performed at the 35th anniversary of *Dreamgirls*. The musical is about a trio of female African American singers. It takes place in the 1960s. Marsai sang with some of the stars of the musical and movie.

Marsai Martin and singer Becky G attended a US women's soccer match in 2019 for Secret deodorant's All Strength, No Sweat campaign.

Marsai is a businesswoman too. In 2019, Marsai and her father started their own movie production company. They named it Genius Productions. They both play a large role in running the company. Marsai's mom, Carol, is the vice president of Genius. The movie deals Marsai handles are worth tens of millions of dollars.

Marsai's film *Little* made $15 million during its opening weekend. It made almost $50 million around the world.

empire: a large group of enterprises or activities led by one person

Marsai has many important responsibilities as an executive producer. That job and her acting endeavors keep her very busy. Marsai is also becoming a social media star. She maintains a channel on YouTube. Viewers get to see Marsai with her family and friends. "I made a channel just so I could show you guys who I am outside of being an executive producer and an actress," she wrote on her YouTube page.

On social media, Marsai is making a name for herself in the world of beauty. In 2018, she started posting beauty **tutorials** on Instagram. They took off. Her beauty tutorials and photos have been viewed by hundreds of thousands of fans.

Marsai attended the 2020 Screen Actors Guild nominations event in Los Angeles. The *Black-ish* team was nominated in 2017 and 2018 for Outstanding Performance by an Ensemble in a Comedy Series.

With the help of stylist Jason Rembert, Marsai is making waves in fashion too. "I find I'm most inspired by clothes that really make a statement," Marsai said in 2019. With bold choices in makeup and fashion, Marsai is inspiring others to express themselves.

tutorial: something, such as a video, that teaches someone how to do something

THE RESPONSIBILITIES OF AN EXECUTIVE PRODUCER

There are many people who work on a film, including an executive producer (EP). The EP has important responsibilities.

The EP starts by having a script written for the film.

Then the EP figures out how much money is needed to make the film. They need to find a studio to pay for it to be made.

The EP hires the director and crew.

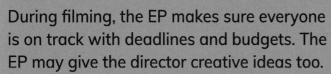

During filming, the EP makes sure everyone is on track with deadlines and budgets. The EP may give the director creative ideas too.

After filming, the EP reviews the film and suggests edits. Then the final cut is made.

work in Progress

Over the years, the cast of *Black-ish* has grown in their relationships and careers together. Marsai said, "We're like a family for sure . . . I feel like I learn something every day—they just make it feel like home, which I love."

In 2019, Marsai and the *Black-ish* cast started filming their sixth season. The same year, the show received the **NAACP** Image Award for Outstanding Comedy Series. It won this award for the fifth year in a row.

Universal Pictures was eager to work with Marsai's production company, Genius Productions. They signed a deal to make a comedy. It is called *StepMonster*. Marsai plays a teenager trying to adjust to life with a new stepmom. In 2019, Universal's president said that the teen "offers a unique perspective as a creator and producer that will **resonate** with all audiences."

Setting up a relationship with Universal was a smart business move. It is leading to many opportunities to produce and act in feature films. Through these jobs, Marsai can advance her message for equality and representation in the media.

By early 2020, Marsai had earned nine awards with the NAACP.

In 2018, Marsai teamed up with DoSomething.org to tackle bullying and social isolation as part of the Treat Yo Friends campaign.

NAACP: the National Association for the Advancement of Colored People; a group that works to end racial discrimination

resonate: to have a strong effect on someone in a personal or emotional way

Giving Back

Like many teens, Marsai shares about her life and her passions on social media. Marsai has used social media to share about her struggles too.

In a 2019 Instagram post, she talked about the pressure she puts on herself to be perfect. She said that this caused her to be "in a dark place" with her feelings.

Marsai sat on the "Powerful with a Purpose" panel during the 2019 Beautycon in Los Angeles.

Marsai asked her followers to talk to loved ones about how they feel and to be themselves. Her post was met with over 200,000 likes. It had more than 2,800 comments of praise and thanks.

Marsai wants to help young people in other ways too. In 2019, she announced the 20/20 Vision **Pledge** with Essilor Lenses. It asks parents to make a pledge to take care of their kids' vision needs. As a child, Marsai had poor vision. It made school and life hard. Once she found the right doctor, her vision problems were solved with glasses. Marsai once felt shy about wearing glasses. But she started owning the look by choosing unique glasses. Now her glasses are a source of empowerment.

SCHOOLING

Marsai and other teen celebrities work long hours. They often have to film shows and movies during the day. This schedule does not allow them to attend regular schools. Stars are often **homeschooled** instead. In 2019, Marsai did three to five hours of school a day to complete eighth and ninth grade classes. She does her learning between shooting scenes for *Black-ish*.

pledge: a promise
homeschool: to learn at home instead of at a school

A Bright Future

Marsai's advice for teens with big dreams is to "just go for it . . . If it is something that you are interested in and it is your passion, then tell your friends, because help is the best thing. If you stay confident, it will happen."

Marsai has had a strong start to her career. And her future looks bright. Kenya Barris has been known to say, "We are all going to be working for her one day."

The teen will keep on running her company with her dad and mom. Marsai also plans to add new titles to her résumé. She plans to be a screenwriter and director. One day, she wants to produce a range of projects, such as reality TV.

As part of her fight for equality and representation, Marsai spoke at the United State of Women Summit in 2018.

Marsai has many projects in the works. As an actress, she plans to continue on *Black-ish*. She is also a part of the show's spin-off, *Mixed-ish*. Plus, Marsai would love to act in a live-action Marvel film in the future.

Under the business partnership with Universal, Marsai is at the forefront of new film productions. This includes an adaptation of a fantasy novel called *Amari and the Night Brothers*. Marsai is also working on a new comedy called *Queen*.

In 2018, Marsai was named one of *TIME* magazine's 25 Most Influential Teens. The title is given to newsworthy teens who receive awards for their work and have a global social media presence.

Teen Strong

Marsai Martin has had many accomplishments in her short career. She has a role on a highly rated show. The teen also creates roles that are not typical in Hollywood.

When accepting the YoungStars award at the 2019 BET Awards, Marsai thanked family, friends, and "the young black girls that inspire me to keep moving forward for them."

Marsai has a strong business mind too. She does what makes sense for her. Marsai fought for what she knew was a smart choice and produced *Little*. She did so despite the advice of her agents. The movie received mixed reviews. But critics and audiences could not deny Marsai's talent.

This young actress has not let her age, gender, or race keep her from her dreams. She hopes to open doors for other kids and teens to make their own films. In all the work she plans to do, Marsai is aiming for it to reflect diversity and equality. The teen shows Hollywood and the world that she is Teen Strong.

ANOTHER RISING STAR

At age 15, Storm Reid was named as one of *TIME*'s most influential teens in 2018. She received the honor for representing diverse characters in the roles she has played. In 2013, at age 10, she was in her first film, *12 Years a Slave*. In 2018, she starred in *A Wrinkle in Time*. Her co-stars included Oprah Winfrey, Reese Witherspoon, and Mindy Kaling. The film was directed by Ava DuVernay. Reid hopes to follow DuVernay's footsteps and be a filmmaker one day.

Timeline

August 14, 2004

Caila Marsai Martin is born in Plano, Texas.

2013

The Martin family moves from Texas to California so Marsai can pursue an acting career.

2014

Marsai starts filming ABC's hit show *Black-ish*. At age 10, she pitches her idea for *Little* to Kenya Barris.

2015

Marsai starts to work as a voice actress on the animated series *Goldie & Bear*.

2016

Marsai first appears on Conan O'Brien's talk show, *Conan*. She plays Melody Ellison in an Amazon special, *An American Girl Story – Melody 1963: Love Has to Win*.

2018

The teen is named as one of *TIME*'s 25 Most Influential Teens.

2020

Marsai wins four NAACP Image Awards for her acting in *Black-ish* and *Little*.

QUIZ

#4
What type of posts did Marsai start on Instagram in 2018?

#1
How old was Marsai when she came up with the idea for *Little*?

#5
What does the 20/20 Vision Pledge ask parents to do?

#2
What were Marsai's first acting jobs?

#6
How many NAACP Image Awards did Marsai win in 2020?

#3
What business did Marsai and her father start in 2019?

6. Four
5. Take care of their kids' vision needs
4. Beauty tutorials
3. A movie production company called Genius Productions
2. Commercials
1. 10

ACTIVITY

Marsai and other teens do not let their age stop them from positively influencing the world around them. Conduct a research project on an influential teen.

MATERIALS

- computer with internet access
- library access
- pencil and paper

STEPS

1. Do an internet search to find the lists of teens named as *TIME*'s 25 Most Influential Teens in the past two years. Choose one teen from the lists.

2. Conduct research about that teen. Find out what makes the teen influential.

3. Take notes as you do your research.

4. Then write an essay about why this teen inspires you. Give specific examples of how the teen is changing the world around them.

GLOSSARY

empire: a large group of enterprises or activities led by one person

empowerment: the process of becoming more confident and taking action for oneself

executive producer: one of the highest positions in media production; may be involved in the production process, or simply oversee it more generally

finance: issues having to do with money and how it is spent or saved

homeschool: to learn at home instead of at a school

NAACP: the National Association for the Advancement of Colored People; a group that works to end racial discrimination

pilot: one episode of a TV show made as a trial run

pitch: to present an idea for a TV show or movie to people who could help pay for it

pledge: a promise

production company: a company that is responsible for developing and filming a specific production, such as a movie or TV show

representation: the process of giving people a voice through better coverage and exposure

resonate: to have a strong effect on someone in a personal or emotional way

talent agency: a company that helps find jobs for actors and other professionals in the entertainment industry

tutorial: something, such as a video, that teaches someone how to do something

READ MORE

Blofield, Robert. *How to Make a Movie in 10 Easy Lessons.* Super Skills. Mission Viejo, CA: Walter Foster, 2015.

Bogle, Donald. *Hollywood Black: The Stars, the Films, the Filmmakers.* Philadelphia, PA: Running Press, 2019.

Furgang, Kathy. *Viola Davis: Actress.* Junior Biographies. New York: Enslow Publishing, 2017.

Gitlin, Marty. *Positive Life Decisions.* Hallandale, FL: Mitchell Lane Publishers, 2018.

Sjonger, Rebecca. *Taking Action to Achieve Equality.* UN Sustainable Development Goals. New York: Crabtree Publishing Company, 2020.

INTERNET SITES

https://www.geniusent.net
Learn more about Marsai and read about what new projects Genius Productions is doing.

https://www.popsugar.com/entertainment/Marsai-Martin-Interview-About-Little-Movie-46043201
Read an interview with Marsai Martin.

https://www.futurelearn.com/courses/film-production/0/steps/12304
Learn more about the different stages of making a film.

https://www.oprahmag.com/entertainment/tv-movies/a27561040/ava-duvernay-hiring-women-hollywood-reporter-interview
Read about director Ava DuVernay and her mission to empower women.

INDEX

ABC 9, 26
Abrams, Stacey 11
agents 8, 9, 12, 25
awards 12, 19, 23, 24, 27

Black-ish 9, 11, 12, 14, 16, 18, 19, 21,
    23, 26, 27
Brown, Miles 9, 10

commercials 7, 9

diversity 5, 13, 19, 23, 25

executive producer 5, 16, 17

Genius Productions 15, 19

homeschool 21

Little 4, 5, 6, 11, 15, 25, 26, 27

parents 7, 8, 11, 21, 23

Reid, Storm 25

sister 7, 10
social media 7, 16, 20, 23

Universal Pictures 19, 23